# FINDING GRANDMAMA GOD

## And Talking Things Over With Her

By Mary Feagan

BALBOA.PRESS
A DIVISION OF HAY HOUSE

Balboa Press books may be ordered through booksellers or by contacting:

Balboa Press
A Division of Hay House
1663 Liberty Drive
Bloomington, IN 47403
www.balboapress.com
844-682-1282

ISBN: 979-8-7652-4205-6 (sc)
ISBN: 979-8-7652-4206-3 (e)

Library of Congress Control Number: 2023908632

Print information available on the last page.

Balboa Press rev. date: 12/13/2023

# Acknowledgements

Thank you, Hal and Sidra Stone, for writing *Embracing Our Selves* and gently explaining how to elicit the unique voices of all our inner selves. Thank you, all my friends – in Atlanta, Winston Salem, Asheville, New York, Bellingham, Tucson, Dublin and St. Louis, and Grandmama God knows where else – for loving me and this book. Thank you, Lynn Wadley, for encouraging me and offering many helpful suggestions. Also thanks, Lynn, for reading so well the part of Grandmama God on the CD. Thank you, Nancy Davis, for cheerleading me on this project for so many years. Thank you, Ellen Hendricks, for collaborating with me as we worked on it on the computer. Thank you, Rev. Dana Winter and Harmony Fellowship, for celebrating Grandmama God with me. And I thank the Unitarian Universalist churches of Atlanta and Wilmington, NC, for offering me classes on feminine spirituality. Finally, thank you, Virginia Morrel and Leigh Allen and everyone who worked on it at Balboa Press, for your gracious support of my book.

# Praise for FINDING GRANDMAMA GOD

"Thanks once again for your delightful and helpful book, <u>Finding Grandmama God</u>. It would be difficult for me to choose between my admiration for the text and the illustrations. I so admire your ability to say so much with <u>line</u>. And thank you for the freeing thoughts and great, deep belly laughs."
– Barb Nobles, my friend

Thanks, first of all for writing <u>Grandmama God</u>. It is so healing. I appreciate your sending four copies up here, and I hope you sell tens of thousands.
– Meg Barnhouse, Unitarian Minister, author of <u>Radio Free Bubba</u>

Mary Feagan embodies in this insightful and wonderful book the modern human struggle to experience the Reality of God. She does it, however, not in stilted theological concepts or with learned philosophical words, but with the startling awareness of her own humanity, sensitively revealed and intimately portrayed. Those who will walk with her through this book will find themselves both refreshed and strengthened. A great book, Mary!
– John Shelby Spong, author, <u>A New Christianity for a New World</u>

Dear Mary, Your manuscript arrived...and we were both very impressed with it....It has a lovely feel to It, and what we read has a very good feeling. Congratulations to you!
– Hal and Sidra Stone, authors, <u>Embracing Our Selves</u>

A touching, enduring and heartfelt book. Many blessings. Treasure yourself.
– Ondrea and Stephen Levine, authors, <u>Embracing the Beloved</u>

I love your <u>Grandmama God</u> book! It's long overdue. Of course the native people of this land have been at it for millennia – you might give them some credit, too. I think you will have a *big audience* (a lot of grandparents for one.) *Go for it*!! Its needed!
– Matthew Fox, author, <u>Original Blessing</u>

# Mary Feagan

A nun for eleven years, I began saying goodbye to Old Judge God as I began to consider leaving the convent. I left in 1968; I was 29 years old. That intimidating concept of God had dominated my life for too long. Then for many years I wandered half-consciously among both old and new concepts of God, not ready to sort out my personal theology. When I was about 50, after two divorces and many confusing relationships with men, one more ruined romance brought me to my knees and to my unfinished business with God. I found I mostly needed a Mother God, and in gently mothering myself, I felt the presence of Grandmama God. Soon I was talking things over with Her. In these conversations, and with a new sense of Granddaddy God as well, I found in my quiet creative times the love I had been longing for. Here is the story behind these poems and illustrations.

# Development of my "Grandmama God"

In the *Phoenix and Dragon* bookstore in Atlanta in 1988, a book fell into my hands from a high shelf. It was Embracing Our Selves, a Voice Dialogue Manual, by Hal and Sidra Stone. I read it in three days. The next summer I spent two weeks at Shakti Gawain's house on the island of Kaua'i. The main workshop leaders were Hal and Sidra, who led voice dialogue sessions every morning. They helped us find, honor and speak from our many selves. I talked from my inner critic, from a marvelous inner pusher who has helped me accomplish many things, from a sweet pleaser, from my sensual woman and from my inner nun who had been very nervous about my life. I also had a fun-loving inner child who loved swimming in the ocean every afternoon and dancing with Gabrielle Roth every evening. Sometime in this process, I noticed I did not have a really loving, nurturing voice inside me.

In 1991 I was living in Myrtle Beach, S.C. A friend who knew of my beginning interest in the Goddess told me about an upcoming weekly course at the Unitarian Universalist Church in Wilmington, N.C., about an hour away. In "Rise Up and Call Her Name" I met ancient images of the Divine Feminine from cultures all around the world. I met Spider Woman and Changing Woman from the native people of my own land. And I met women like myself who longed for images of a Mother God. I began writing about them in my journal.

In my personal life, I was recovering from what I hoped was my last impulsive, ungrounded relationship. I finally saw that I was not the strong sensible partner of another "poor baby." I was a "poor baby," too. Then mothering myself became my highest priority. Effortlessly, that mothering turned into grandmothering, perhaps because I have seen so much love in grandmothers. As I found the loving voice of the Divine Feminine in me and turned to Her in all the events of my life, Grandmama God came alive in me.

# My New Thoughts on God

My new thoughts about God, still in formation, are about the mysteries of being, loving and creating. God is the beginning and ongoing source of everything. God is the energy in everyone and everything. God is present in everyone and everything, like light in a light bulb. God is "I AM." Because I also am, I participate in God. Of course, the same goes for everyone and everything that exists. God is a supportive, impersonal power that infuses everything and loves it into being. The love and delight of God is woven into support for everyone's existence. God is Love, and is in us as our love for ourselves, for one another and for the earth. Love inspires making, creating, gift-giving, and love infuses anything made, anything given. God is presence, being, source, energy, love, creativity, giving, wherever they are found. In our being, loving and creating, we are continuing God, extending God. In our being, loving and creating, we evolve God.

Now in things there are usually two poles, as in time, day and night; in electricity, positive and negative; in living things, masculine and feminine. God is, of course, the source of this twoness. God has two sides, a creative making and doing side, and a holding, loving, being side. So I have images I call Granddaddy and Grandmama God. I have them because my mind uses images to think with. I remember they denote what is far beyond images. I have consciously chosen to chance my image of the masculine side of God from an old judge to a loving grandfather. I talk with Granddaddy God often. He is an archetype, a universal image which is in my imagination. He is also an energy, a felt power in the universe, which is in me as one of my inner selves.

However, it was the feminine side of God I had missed all my life. So I talk mostly with Her in this book. When I talk with Grandmama God, I am talking with the loving feminine side of God, found in me because I am part of God. Grandmama God is also a self of mine, like my inner child or my artist or my businesswoman. Of course, I don't make these distinctions when I have conversations with Her. I want to remember union, remember oneness. I love it when I lose all these thoughts and just be in wonder, in wordless awe. But words sustain me in-between times.

# Table of Contents

## Longing for a Homecoming

Granddaddy God, did you put this longing in my heart?

I know You did it. It has made me do crazy things

Like shop twenty days for the perfect socks for that dress,

Like have what's-his-name for my boyfriend,

Like buy the house on Cardinal Lake

and then shop so much I was never home.

This longing feels sort of like homesickness.

That's just it. My heart wants to feel at home.

My heart wants a homecoming.

Granddaddy God, I've been longing so long.

I want some ease, some measure of satisfaction. Please.

"Mary," says Granddaddy God.

"My Child, my Precious One, my Love.

Yes, I helped give that longing to you,

But I don't much handle the joy of My daughters.

It's not that I can't, and don't get Me wrong,

My own joy is as full as a bucket of well water.

But you need a woman to help you, My dear one, My daughter.

Go to Grandmama God now. She knows how you feel.

She knows what your heart feels from the inside, and

She's good at homecomings. She's been waiting for you."

"Hush, Child," She says, as She hugs me and holds me.

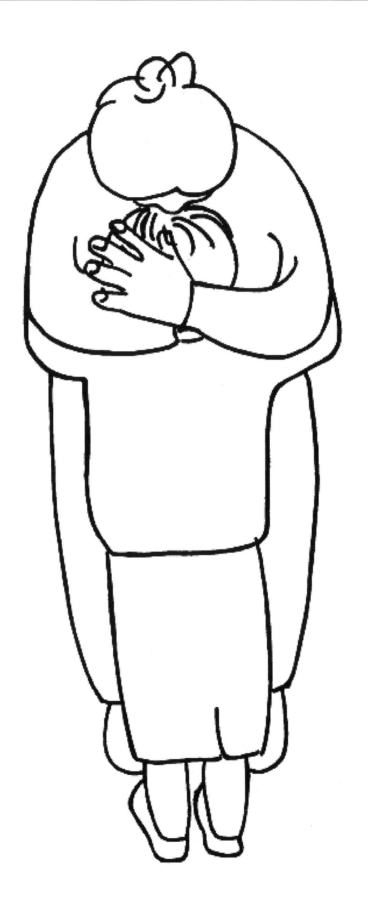

## I Feel Like I'm Stuck in the First Grade

I feel like I'm stuck in the first grade.

I want, intend, insist I have let go

That stupid old petty old mean Old Judge God.

I learned him in the first grade.

And my first grade scared self has stayed stuck with him there.

Wish I could just let them be, him and little scared me.

Little girl-child in me I once was,

I'll just love you and let you be.

Silly old mean Old Judge

God, I'll just let you be.

I'll hold you both, love you both,

as parts of me I made.

I'm ready for life in the second grade.

## Old Judge God Did the Best He Could

For years I've been fussing at Old Judge God.

I've sent Him away a million times,

But he always came back.

He was the only God I had,

And he knew it.

Now I know he did the best he could.

He kept me safe and warm the best he could,

While we both waited for me to find Grandmama God.

## I Thought God Wanted My Constant Attention

I thought God wanted my constant attention.

I thought God wanted me to burn continual candles in his honor.

No, I thought God needed me to burn myself like I was

About as valuable as an old Family Dollar candle.

I thought God wanted, no, demanded me to squelch my pleasures,

Sit on my dreams, dry up my juices, to save my spiritual ass.


Now come to find out that my old god was just a bad dream.

Come to find out the real God, near as I can figure out,

The real God wants me to give myself a fair amount of attention.

Boy, howdy! The real God just told me to light twelve candles in my honor

And parade naked in the house with my Easter hat on.

I think I'm going to like listening to this God.

## You Damn Old God-Fraud, Go Away

You damn old God-Fraud, go away.

I've been trying to get out from under you too long.

I've been praying to you for sweet things, you bitter old sourpuss.

No wonder my apples were rotten, my dreams became nightmares.


Today I closed my eyes while I showered.

I reached in a corner for the soap –

It was gone.

Then I opened my eyes and saw I had been

reaching in the wrong corner.

Damn you.

Praying to you was like reaching in the wrong corner.

There was nobody there.


I'm going to be very careful now which God I pray to.

And when I'm careful, you God-Fraud, it won't be you.


You can't tell me you exist.

Because you don't.

I know that. But my mind doesn't.

You may, God help me,

Always have a place in my mind.

Then oh, God really help me,

Help me find a place for you in my heart.

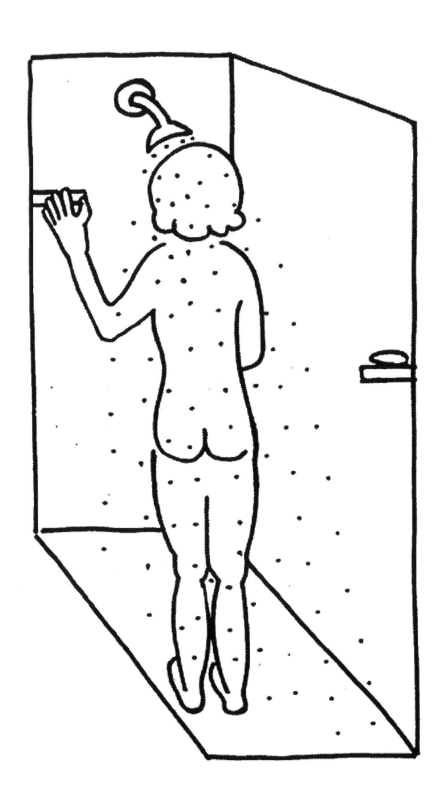

## Talking to My Old Judge God

Listen, My Old Judge God, I want to be free from you.

I want to be free to have fun and be rich, too.

But I'm afraid you will hurt me if I do.

I think you are a bully.

Are you a bully who takes care of me,

Like a Mafia godfather?

Maybe I can buy your favor

With special candles and holy water.

When I went in the convent,

I thought your favor cost my life.

Now I hope you've come down in price.

Anyway, come to think of it,

I don't want to pay you at all.

I want to be free from you.


Old Judge God, you aren't really God.

I created you a long time ago in catechism class.

You are in my mind as a strict

Hardhearted sourpuss Scrooge.

But now I want to know the truth.

Did you like being my god?

Are you sad or glad I want to be free?

Tell me, please. I need to know.

Maybe you can help me let you go.


"Mary, I played the role you gave me.

But it was hard to be so constantly hardhearted.

I'm ready to put down this judging job.

Sometimes I used to like it, but

Now I want to stop playing God.

I'm tired, Honey I'm worn out.

I'm glad you want to be free from me.

I want to be free, too. I want to retire.

I thank God it's the end.

Now I want to be your, well, let's say

Your uncle, your friend."

## Old Judge God Says

My God, Girl, I've been waiting all your life
For this. It feels like Christmas morning.
You finally have the courage to let me go.
Just for the record, let me say a few words.
I'm so excited, I won't be walking,
I'll be dancing away.
I've been stuck in your fear, too, you know.
Now I can grow in wisdom and joy,
Grow in usefulness, too. Of course,
I'm not really going away. Like a snake
Changes his skin and lives in a new one,

I'll take off my dark robe and wear a
Sky blue one, or one made of flowers.
I'll still be a judge for you when you ask me,
Only now you'll be the boss. You'll see.
Being good, Honey, is so lovely, it glows,
When fear's gone. Now I'm telling you,
Be good to yourself, fill your senses.
Now you need beauty, Mary, and you need play.
I want you to open your wings and fly high
Like a bird. Soon you'll have fresh images
Of God that you'll love. Mark my word.

But for now, just be angry at me for a while.
And be mad at those old lessons you learned
About me when you were a child. You were lied to.
Now you stomp on the beach and you shout at the clouds.
I'm for truth, too. So go ahead, Girl. Get angry out loud.

### You Old Judge God, Get Off My Back

You Old Judge God, get off my back

"Mary, why don't you just put me down?"


Damn it, Old Judge God, get off my back

"Mary. Mary. I'm off. I'm gone."

## I Exorcise You, Old Judge God

I exorcise you, you mean Old Judge God.
I exorcise you, you god who played favorites,
        who liked the cute girls best.
I exorcise you, you pitiful old god,
        who wanted the sweets of children in lent,
        who scared them in confession,
        who let the team with the most prayers win.
You were too little, too easily bought.

I thought the nuns told the truth when the said
        you liked nuns best of all.
Oh, I guess they did, considering who you are.
The poor nuns, at least the unhappy ones,
        had just believed the same lies I had.
For I once believed your petty jealousy,
        your Puritan possessiveness,
        your lack of appreciation of a good party.
I am especially mad that I believed your lack of appreciation
        of a private bedroom party.

I exorcise you, you stupid old
        low-down old false Old Judge God.
I'm glad you never existed. Get out.
Go. Good riddance. Goodbye.

## That Old Judge God Is Walking Away

That Old Judge God is walking away.
He's finished now. I guess He was as much
God as I could imagine at the time.
I used to think that Old Judge God
Didn't want me to have you.
Now I know he never even existed.
Well, he's walking away now. I see Him
Shuffling down a dirt road.
He's dragging a ragged black robe
Behind his bare sagging ass.

I'm ready for Grandmama God now.
I'm ready for big-hearted, big-breasted Grandmama God.
I'm ready for Grandmama God, bigger than fourteen skies,
Bigger than the color orange expanded out beyond all directions,
Bigger than my longing for fullness multiplied to forty zillion,
Bigger than my feeling of fullness when I am
Dancing with you, and everyone we know
Is clapping stars to us.

## Granddaddy God, I'm Just Finding You

Granddaddy God, I'm just finding You.

I want to know You free and clear

Of my old fear of Old Judge God.

When I left him, I left You, too.

Now I'm finding You, strong, generous, faithful,

Full of love, fresh as dew.

I'm grateful for every grace that leads me on to You.

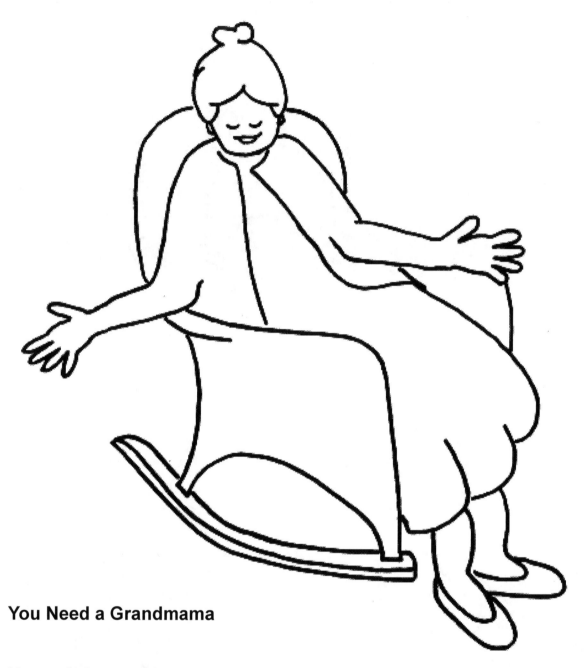

## You Need a Grandmama

I know what you need,

'Cause I'm beginning to know what I need.

I mean deep down the one basic thing,

Before money and house and romance and food and friends.

You need to find, create from nothing if you have to,

Find the loving mama in yourself.

Find the mama who hasn't a bad thing in the world to say about you.

Maybe she's your grandmama,

Your ever-loving-longing-to-rock-you-grandmama.

She is alive somewhere deep down in you,

And she loves you mightily with her big old soft warm loving heart.

And oh, she wants you to hear her.

She's not loud but she's steady as a 'lectric clock tick-tocking,

Talking love for your sweet special self. You listen to her.

Most of all you need to listen to her.

Then say what she says. Repeat her words.

You are loved beyond your wildest dreams.

You are precious and wonderful, and you can do the job.

And you're safe with her, you're safe.

She'll hold you tight when the bad times seem to come.

She's full of the Spirit, and she knows you're full of the Spirit, too.

She reminds you all the time that the Spirit is just love, Honey.

Sweet and simple homegrown love. She'll help you feel that love in you,

And she'll help you pass it on. Listen to her.

Most of all you need to listen to her. Stay close to her.

Let her rock your soul all day. Let her croon to you,

Tuck you in, put you to gentle sleep at night. You need your very own

Holding-you-rocking-you-loving-you-all-the-time grandmama.

## Grandmama God

I'm sometimes think I'm creating Her from nothing.
But that isn't true.
She came to me and I felt Her.
I have felt Her holding me when I cried,
And I have felt Her walking with me at the edge of the ocean.
I have felt Her most nights in the quiet dark before I slept.
When I am with a real loving grandmother like Mrs. Hardee,
Who hugs unfamiliar children and holds my hand,
I feel Her. I feel Her.

I call Her "Grandmama God."

She is the Heart of the universe.
You could call Her the Goddess of the universe,
And I sometimes do.
But "Grandmama God" brings me right into heaven's kitchen
With warm biscuits and butter and strawberry jam.
She is just love, loving to give Herself away.

## Grandmama God, May I Call You That?

Grandmama God, may I call You that?
Or would You prefer another name?
I could call You "Grandmother God," or
I could call you "God the Mother."
Of course, lots of people call You "Goddess"
But I like "Grandmama God" Best.

"Darling Mary, you know what your own dear
Mother is called by her grandchildren.
They call her 'Mamere,'
and she loves it.
I love 'Grandmama God'
Because My grand girl calls Me that."

## The True God Loves Me Wildly

The true God,
Like a grandmama,
Loves me wildly.
She wants me exuberant,
Rich, sexy, healthy.
She holds my hand
And leads me to the dance floor.

## This is for John, Who Feels Left Out

John, I just found my long-lost Grandmama God.
No, I was long lost, and She found me.
Come join in the celebration.
You'll like Her.
Come to the family reunion.

I'm so happy, and
I want you at the party.
Granddaddy God will be there.
He's proud of Her, and
He's relieved.
He didn't much like being God alone.
Besides, He delights in our loving Her, and
He especially likes family reunions.

You come too, John.

## Grandmama God Invites Me

I've just noticed another bad habit –

My thinking I need to please Grandmama God.

I treat Her like I used to treat of Old Judge God,

As though She's demanding and wants lots of praise.


Grandmama God is an old potter woman.

Humming, hands steady, legs spread,

She throws countless bowls on Her wheel.

She is the Beauty that gives birth to all forms.

She is the joy of constant creation.


Has she any need for a dutiful daughter?

Does She want my praise or my fearful attention?

She's the moon's reach from wanting.


She invites me, however.

She invites me to think myself free from old habits.

She invites me to give birth to fresh, beautiful forms.

She gives me some clay and says, laughing,

"Here you are. Create a new world.

## Grandmama God Rocks My Soul

Grandmama God wants to rock my soul.

She waits and waits for me to sit still.

Sometimes I cry first.

Then She holds me and lets me,

Ahh, She lets me ease into peace.

Then She breathes me.

That's the only way I can say it.

She holds me so I breathe from my belly to my hair.

For the first time all day, my soul comes in my body.

And as I breathe, Grandmama God rocks my soul.

## Grandmama God, What About Sex?

Grandmama God, what about sex?
Should I want it? Do you bless it?
May I have some? What's it for?

"Mary, My child, shhh, Child.
Slow down and feel the buzzing in your head.
Then feel the buzzing in your body.
Feel the buzzing between your legs, too.
That buzz is sexual, Honey, it's life itself.
You are alive, daughter of Mine.
You are alive because of sex.
You are alive because of wanting.
Your are alive because of desire,
Because of longing, because of yearning.

You are alive because your mama and your daddy
Were each lonely by themselves.
They wanted connection, union, communion.
Sex is the celebration of folks' longing for union.
And it's continual communion too,
If you dare to live in ecstasy.

Mary, My daughter, ask me another question.
You know, the question all daughters dream of asking.
Don't be shy, Girl, I want to tell you."

Grandmama God, please, do you ever have sex?

"Oh, Mary, Granddaddy God and I live in continual communion.
We live in ecstasy. We are that ecstasy.
We are that love, that sex, that exuberant meeting.
Every minute, every second, We find each other
In the dark and come together.
Every minute, Mary, every second, sparks fly and
Stars are born as We unite in joy.
Granddaddy God and I, why, come to think of it,
Sex is all we ever do."

## Grandmama God, Today I Want You To Rock My Soul

Grandmama God, I want You to rock my soul.
But I don't need Your sweet comforting right now.
Today I want You to rock and roll with me.
I want to dance all day with You.

I used to go to Old Judge God with my misery and pain,
Sometimes I suffered good as Jesus, or I tried to.
When times were good, I thanked Him with guilty gratitude
And ran before He took my joys away.

Well, I'm doing different with Him now.
But that's another poem.
Now I'm talking to You, Grandmama God.
I want to dance all day with You.

Grandmama God, I know You love to dance.
You slow danced yesterday in the ocean waves.
Wild times, too, You dance Your heart out in the sea.
Today I want to dance all day with You.
Fish dance You. Dolphins dance You. Stars dance You, too.
You dance in the moving moon, Grandmama God.
You dance in the wild and gentle wind.
Please dance in me all day today.

My cat Gracie dances with her string around the kitchen chairs.
My typewriter dances the words to make this poem.
Well, Grandmama God, today I want to dance my thanks to You.
I want to dance all day with You.

No guilt, no sneaky joy. No more.
Just rock me in the waves and winds and stars.
Today I want to dance all day with You.
My joy is full 'cause You are dancing, too.

## Take Me Down, Grandmama God

Take me down, Grandmama God.
Take me down under.
Take me down, Grandmama God,
Under my fear of aloneness.
Take me down, Grandmama God,
Under money and mortgages and mortality.
Take me down, Grandmama God,
Under my body's ache for a loving partner.
Take me down, Grandmama God,
Under my soul's ache for order and beauty.
Take me down, Grandmama God,
Under all my judgments of myself.
Take me down, Grandmama God,
Under my bone weariness tonight.
Take me down, Grandmama God,
Into the earth, Your womb, Your cradle.
Take me down, Grandmama God,
Into Your warm arms.
Hold me, Grandmama God, hold me.

## Grandmama God, May I Go to the Mall?

"Oh, Honeychild, you keep asking Me permissions.
It's OK, ask Me often as you like.
But here's the truth:
I want you to have fun, feel free,
Play in the sun, laugh, dance.
I know you'll work, so we won't worry about that.
I'm not so sure you'll play.

So, child, if going to the mall is fun for you,
I want you to go.
If it wearies you, find a better way to play.
I'll go with you wherever you go.
I'll love you, whatever you do.
But I'm warning you, Love,
If we go the mall together,
Be prepared to spend some money on yourself.
I want you to have some beautiful new clothes.
I want you to have clothes fit for a goddess."

## Grandmama God Went to the Mall Tonight

Grandmama God went to the mall tonight.
You know I call Her Grandmama God,
And you may think I'm crazy
Or even blasphemous
But I don't care. She was there.
We went shopping together.

She told me to get something beautiful for myself.
I asked Her what she thought of the raspberry cotton sweater.
She told me I looked like a goddess in it.
She should know.
"Only get what purely delights you," She whispered.
I bought the sweater and thought it was enough.

She told me, "Let's just look some more.
We'll see what else might please you, Honey.
I found a necklace I loved but didn't need.
Grandmama God said, "You'll have fun with it.
Don't think twice. Just buy it."

I loved shopping with Her.
She gave me courage to give myself gifts
After a long winter.
She kept me calm, even lighthearted.
We celebrated beauty together at the mall.

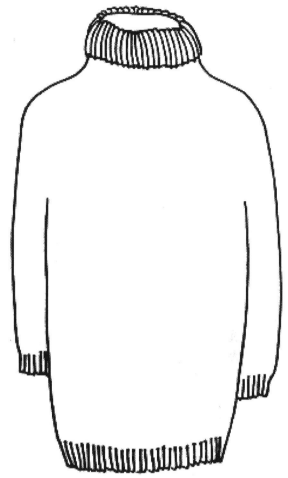

Sometimes when I have shopped alone
I've come home late and empty-handed.
I was scared to make a mistake,
Scared to spend money, scared to make a choice.
I was scared to displease that Old Judge God,
For I still had my old notions about him.

But tonight was different.
Tonight Grandmama God and I went shopping together.
And a miracle happened right there at the mall.
I had fun shopping.

## Grandmama God, Help Heal the Bitter Child In Me

Grandmama God, please help heal the bitter child in me.
I just found her tonight. She's been in me all along, of course,
Whining and moaning and groaning.
Here's what she always says:
"I never get any," or "I got left out in the rain."
"I got less, as usual." "You forgot about me again, and now
It's too late, anyway."

And whenever a child at school talks like my bitter child,
I get cross-eyed, stuck and crazy.
Grandmama God, tell me something wise about her.
Help me love her. Help me heal her.
Help me love the bitter children.

And Grandmama God says, "Mary, let me talk to her awhile.
"Little one," says Grandmama God, "I love you.
I've been loving you all along.
You've been getting the richest love around.
The stars, the moon, the sun, the earth,
I wound them up for your delight.
I offer them all to you again today.
Please take My gifts. Please take My love.
I give you the dearest person who loves you,
Mary. She would dance on her head to give you joy."

What are you scared of, Honeychild?"
"Grandmama God, I'm scared I won't be different.
I'll get lost in the love. I don't want to be like all the others."

"Oh, Sweetie," says Grandmama God, "You are you,
Not because you are bitter.
You'll always be your own true self,
Even more when you feel loved.
Truly, I promise you'll be even more yourself when
You've let go all the sourness and
Opened the sweet gifts from Mary and Me."
"But who will I be, Grandmama God? I've only been bitter."

Go down under that, Child. Can you find your heart?"

"Yes, Grandmama God, but it feels small, cold, shriveled and hard,
Like a little old raisin lost under the rug."

"Oh, Sugar, give it to Me. I'll warm it. I'll help to grow big and strong,
Soft and beautiful, like a fat ripe strawberry."

"But Grandmama God, what will I do?
And if I don't complain, won't Mary be hurt?"

"No, Love, guarding Mary was never your job.
You're just a child.
Mary has a protector who'll keep her from danger.
Your real job stays the same as it's been:
Ask for what you want;
Say how you feel; and,
And this makes all the difference –
Mind your manners.
Say 'Please' when you want something,
'No, thank you' when you don't,
And say a heartfelt 'Thank you'
When your mama's sweet to you.
Thank Me, too, as you find My gifts."

"It feels funny, Grandmama God, not to be bitter.
Will You help me keep it gone?
Will You help me keep my heart like a fat strawberry?"

"I will, Darling Child,
Polite Child of My heart."

"Thank You, Grandmama God.
And thank you, Mama, for worrying about me."

## "Make a Home for Your Heart," Says Grandmama God


"Make a home for your heart," says Grandmama God.

"I'll help you build it, My Girl, with your love and your dreams."


Thank You, Grandmama God. Let's see.


My home for my heart has a lake near it,

A Saturday morning gray-green lake.

My home for my heart has the sky over it,

A wide blue sky with wild white clouds.

My home for my heart has my man in it,

    With the soul of a poet and light, dancing feet.

My home for my heart has my family in it,

    Playing Pictionary and laughing.

My home for my heart has Margie and Sloane in it,

    And Molly, and Melinda and Keith,

    And Ceilidh, and all my dear friends.

My home for my heart has two cats in it,

    Charming ones named Gracie and Bud.

My home for my heart has a Scottish Terrier in it,

    Who sleeps at my feet and dreams of me.

My home for my heart has me in it,

    Writing and drawing, dreaming and dancing.

My home for my heart smells like birthday cake in the oven.

My home for my heart is full of flowers and the sound of violins.

My home for my heart lives in the heart of Grandmama God.

## Grandmama God, Please Hold the Baby

I'm worrying about money, Grandmama God.

I'm in bed thinking how much it's going

    to cost to have gutters put on.

I'm fearing the cleaning service will charge me a lot

    to clean the whole house.

So please hold the baby.

My mind is a fretful tangle of dollar signs

    and ladders and cobwebs.

Wait a minute, Grandmama God.

How about You take the worries?

Then I can hold the baby.

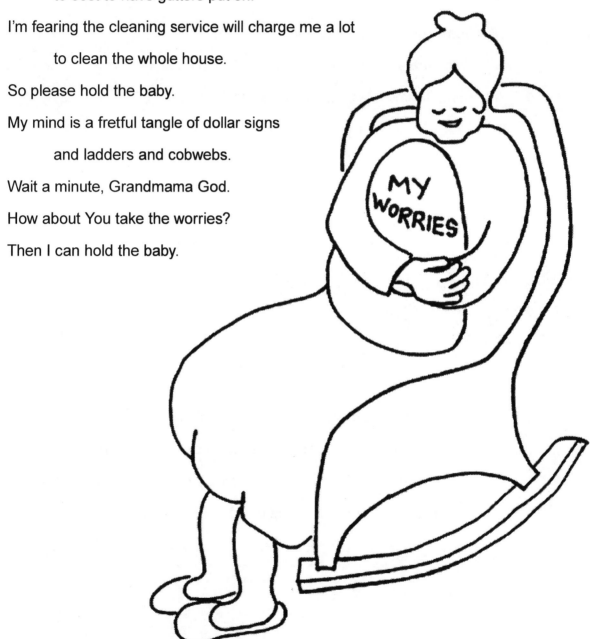

## Thank You, Grandmama God

Thank You, Grandmama God,
For holding me last night while
I tossed and turned
And thought and lost
About an hour of sleep,
Wanting to solve
This summer's puzzle.
I'd tell You the details,
But you've heard me say them
A hundred times already.
Anyway, thank You.
I felt You holding me.
You just held onto me.
When I lay on my left side,
You were behind me.
When I turned on my back,
You were under me.
When I squirmed on my right side,
You stayed with me. You told me,
"It'll be all right. It'll all work out."
You held me tight
All through the night.
No worry was too absurd.
I relaxed in Your arms.
Your sweet words relaxed my soul.
"I love you even
When you worry," You said.
It was the sweetest worrying
I've ever done.
Thank You, Grandmama God.

## "Don't Deal With Future Hands," Says Grandmama God

"Don't deal with future hands," says Grandmama God.
"Hey, My Mary, Girl, today is your game.
Play it with passion.
I've dealt you four aces today, Darling.
The ocean, azaleas, the sweet breeze, the birds.
No, more like twenty-nine aces I've dealt you,
Counting your friendships and talents and
So much more I could say.
Now, play.

Don't peek into the future,

Trying to see your hand, say,

On May twenty-third.

Just play out today.

Breathe deeply, put on flute music,

Call your mother, wash clothes,

Sort mail, and then

Stop and feel your heart, Girl.

Then feel your suspense

For what's next.

But don't crane your neck looking

Into the future.

Just win today's game.

Now, play.

You can play all your aces, Mary, and

I'll just give you more, for

This game is in My casino.

Honey, you're not playing against the house.

I'm the Queen here. I own the house,

And you're My daughter.

There's no one against you.

You can't lose if you play.

So relax, laugh, and take chances.

The best game you can play's called 'today.'"

## A New Way to Pray

"Mary, My Girl, you're ready to learn

A new way to pray.

Today I'm going to teach you to pray.

Are you ready?"


Yes, Grandmama God, I want to learn

to pray your way.


"OK, Mary, come inside your body.

Feel your arm on your belly.

Feel the tingle in your toes.

Feel your breath in your nose.

Feel it as it fills your chest.

Then let it out again and rest.

Feel your whole body buzz and glow.


That's prayer, My Girl.

Trust and let go."

## Grandmama God, What About Compassion?

Grandmama God, what about compassion?
What about pity for poor children?
What about sadness for the homeless?
I say I feel sorry for them.
What I mean is, I feel their fear, their panic,
        their loneliness and lostness.
Then my heart almost breaks and I turn away.

"My Dear Child, My Love, come to Me.
You're feeling lonely and lost now, that's all.
You give those folks feelings they may never have.
In the course of a day they, like you,
May feel thousands of ways.
You only can know what you feel, Sweetie.
Shhh, settle down. Let Me hold you.
Let's talk about you.

So you're scared today, Sugar, and unsure of yourself?
You need to mother yourself well.
Shhh, breathe. Sit a spell.
You are loved, Honeychild, by so many friends.
Your family loves you, too.
But you can't feel it now, Dear.
It's OK.
Shhh. I know what to do.
Hold yourself still, Mary. Hold your heart.
Just love yourself. Honest.
Just as you are, feeling
Pitiful, lonely, lost, poor and scared.

*You aren't those ways always, but you feel those ways now.*
*So feel them fully. They'll take you through*
*To new feelings. Feel them well now.*
*Have compassion on your own*
*Poor old dear sad homeless self today.*
*Tomorrow when you feel better,*
*Ask Me again about poor folks."*

## Grandmama God, Help Me Feel Your Sweet Mothering Today

Grandmama God, help me feel Your sweet mothering today.

I want little me to feel loved and safe.

I would tell You I feel creepy and scared,

But those aren't the feelings I want to keep.

I'll get quiet now. Thank God You're here.

I can hear You say in my ear,

"Shhh, breathe deeply, Love. Rest.

I'm here now. You're safe. You're home.

What's best for you will come.

You are deeply loved.

You have all you need, and more.

You don't have to go banging on door after door

To find your next move.

Have faith in life's flow.

Let your future grow gently

From today's thoughts and cheer.

This is not a <u>mean</u>while,

It's a <u>sweet</u> while.

So relax, Child.

I'm your Grandmama God. I'm here."

## Grandmama God, Here's My Main Question

Grandmama God, here's my main question:
Is it rude to dance before
The depressed and the dying?
May I flaunt my joy,
Hold it large, keep it flying?

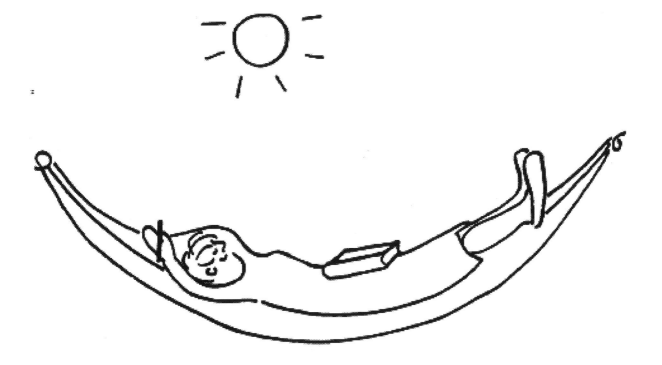

## "Put Down Your Pen," Says Grandmama God

"Put down your pen," says Grandmama God
"Breathe.
Relax.
Feel the sun
On your face.
Stop the race
To get things done.
Everything is in place.
Everything is OK.
For twenty minutes it can stay just so
While you play,
While you pray, while you stay with Me."

## Grandmama God, Help Me Slow Down

Grandmama God, help me slow down.
I've been rushing around again.
Elise told me I'm like the white rabbit in
Alice in Wonderland.
Oh, dear. She's right.
It feels like a bad habit.
Nothing's urgent, is it?

"My darling Mary, there is one thing urgent.
Urgent, My Love, urgent.
It's urgent that you love your dear self.
Everything else will come with ease, then.
No need to rush around, so much need to love--
Love yourself first.
When you hear a police siren
Or see a fire truck, remember
The one urgent thing,
And slow down so your heart can love you."

## Grandmama God Asks Me About Jody

"Honey, tell Me about Jody.
Why did it bother you so much, that
He ate the popcorn before he drew his picture?"

I'll try to find out, Grandmama God.
My selves, which of you hated it the most,
When he ate the popcorn?

"I did. I'm the Righteous One. The Fair Deal One.
I'm the one who measures, judges, allots pure justice.
Things are black and white with me.
You gave him a fair consequence for no work:
No finished picture, no popcorn.
Clear and simple. Perfect.
Then the nervy guy quick-swiped two pieces.
Outrageous, bold insubordination.
He ought to be hung by his heels.

I love fair cases, good classes, and clean consequences.
I love law and order, but mostly I love order. Mine.
Jody flipped my order upside down
and for a moment ran my show.
It was as though he'd snapped my whip in two."

Oh, Grandmama God, teach me to love Jody
More than I love order.
Help me give the Righteous One a new job--
See the most amazing order in my classes;
See the order of our faithfulness to Art;
See the order of our love for one another.

## I Want High Expectations and No Pity

Grandmama God, I know You want me to find and trust my own desires.
And now you're asking me again just what I want.
It's not comforting, thank You, at least not today.

At school, where I am the most, I most want for my students
High expectations and no pity.
I want to be wise and fair, ruthless and happy,
Whether the kids are good or bad.
Ms. Mary Sweetness in me needs a partner.
Maybe Ms. Mary Sourness?
At least, Ms. Mary Serious.

Aha. Here's what I want.
Permission, ways to take care of myself,
Even at the kids' expense.
Really. I want to enforce my rules.
Period. No excuses, no pity.
No second and third chances.
But you know what? It's mostly
One rule I want kept, which is
That children don't shout out stuff to me.
That irritates my very heart and soul.
Why does it grate on me so much?
Well, because I have no consequence for it.
I pay for it myself with my own stillborn stress.
To tell You the truth, What irritates me most
Is the calling out of a kid named Jimmy Gilmore.
He stutters, so my pity-button gets pushed, too.
Oho. Oh, no, he doesn't get my pity any more.

Grandmama God, thank you for listening.
I received three gifts from that.
The two I know are that I want a sidekick for Ms. Sweetness,
And that I want justice for little Jimmy Gilmore.
*Let's see...What is the third?*
*Perhaps it's that I found I have a sense of humor*
*I can use when kids call out or otherwise are bad.*

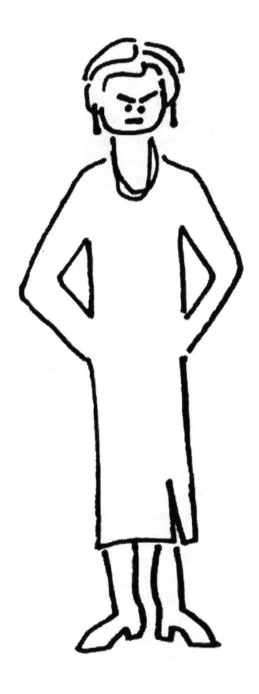

## "Be Cold-Blooded in Peace," Says Grandmama God

Grandmama God, help me.
When I scold a child at school,
The scared child in me cries.
She feels the terror of her own near death.
She cringes when I'm loud or merely stone-cold sober.
Of course, I can't be only nice, so I come home
With a scared child on my shoulders.
I'm all worn out with ten more weeks of school.
Please help me, Grandmama God.

"My dearest daughter, you tell the truth.
You understand your selves so well.
Your scared child meets your cold mad woman,
And the young one gets hysterical.
She feels her life's in danger.
You need to fuss and fume at those kids now and then,
And those hot children need some icy orders.
Talk to them about it. Teach them
What you want your inner child to know.
Teach them you're both warm and frozen-blooded;
They're both OK. Just let them know
You can be sun and rain, fog and snow.
And they're safe, even loved, in all your weathers.

They can keep their own child hearts safe
And so can you, your child's.
Teach them. Your own child needs to hear it."

## Last Night I Dreamed I Kissed a Girl with AIDS

Last night I dreamed I kissed a girl with AIDS.
She was dear to me and we hadn't met in a long time.
She was a young black woman with skin the color of
   cream-in-your-coffee.
I was so glad to see her.
We kissed, a slightly wet kiss, even.
Then another young woman behind me said,
"What if she has AIDS?"
My dear friend looked at me sheepishly and said,
"I do."

I immediately fretted up a storm of worries about myself.
Only now, awake, do I wonder about her.
That must be the way out of fretting,
Feel what the other one must feel,
Worry a bit about her.
More awake now, I know those kissing women both were me,
Healthy me and sick me.
Healthy me wants to turn her back on my sick pathetic self.
But the love is there between them.
Either sick me gets well or she dies.
In either case, I guess, healthy me lives on.
She can't die.
Could my pathetic self again run all my life?
No way, I can reassure my healthy self.

Who is this sick self, anyway?
Can her role, her job, be changed?
That really asks, "Can she be cured of AIDS?"
But AIDS is, of course, symbolic.

So what disease has this self got
That I dreamed up as AIDS?
I'd say she had a chronic case of pity.
Pity for pitiful people, basically.
Pagan babies, stray puppies, all poor fools,
Not knowing she needs her pity most of all.
She's had pity for most others, and with it, sneering contempt.
Pity and self-righteousness.
She's either got to die or give these up.
For simplicity, let's just say righteous pity.
Without it, who would she be?
It seems her very essence.

"No, her essence is love and light, Child,"
Says Grandmama God.
"Believe it. Remember it.
That's why she can live and bloom.
The righteous pity was just her first attempt at loving.
It's not her last.
She's been the part of you
That's scared to give your heart away.
She's easing out of her fears
Like a too-fat seed lifts off its husk.
Give her time and darkness.
She'll soon be glad to leave those old small ways.
Her own natural love will heal her,
And your love helps her heal.
Trust Me. She's safe to kiss now.
In fact, since real love is catching, kiss her well."

## "Listen to Your Child," Says Grandmama God

"My daughter, you're the mama of yourself, you know.
You've been dealing with your house
And your clothes and your friends.
Stop all that now. Slow yourself down.
Hush now and listen to your child.
Ask her what she wants. Then shhh. Listen.
Today is for the child."

And so I say,
What do you want today, My darling daughter?

"Mama, I'd like honey on a banana for breakfast.
And then I want to make mud pies, wearing only my underpants.
And I want to play hide-n-seek with Nancy."

My dear child, I'll give you
A banana dripping in honey for breakfast.
I'll serve you breakfast in the bathtub, Darling,
And drip honey all over you, too.
You may make hundreds of mud pies today, My child.
I'll call Nancy's mama, and Mike's mama.
I'll call Julie and Meryl's mama too, if you like.
Today we'll have a mud pie party.
While the mud pies bake in the sun, I'll hose you all clean.
Then you can play hide-and-seek till dinner.
How does that sound to you, My Girl?

"It all sounds perfect, Mama. Thank you."

Now tell me, Pumpkin, what you'd like for lunch.

## "Get your Doll, Honey," Says Grandmama God

"Get you doll, Honey."

Get the damn doll?
Oops, excuse me, Grandmama God,
It's just that I was ready to do seventeen things.

"Get your doll, Honey, and a cup of hot cider.
Come sit in the rocker with Me."

But I was going to call Nancy
And then go grocery shopping.
Surely you know we're out of bananas.

"Get your doll and cider,
And sit in the rocker with Me.
You hold the doll like I'm holding you.
You stroke her hair and I'll stroke yours.
You rub her tummy and I'll rub yours.
Really.
Just rock and stroke her.
Then drink some cider.
Relax. Breathe deeply. Let go.
Let go into My arms.
Let go into My everlasting love.
If this is hard, you know
How much you need it.
Honey, get back in that chair."

Oh, Grandmama God, help me let You rock me.

## I Ask Grandmama God About Pleasure

What about play, Grandmama God?
What about fun?
What about mindless hilarious laughter?
What about delicious pleasures?
What about even juicy wet kisses?
Really, Grandmama God, what about sex?
Tell me. Please tell me.
I did it behind Old Judge God's back
Before I knew You and Granddaddy God.
Now I don't do it, waiting for the stars to be in perfect positions.
While the stars are lining up, Grandmama God, tell me.

"Honey, there's a fire roaring in you fireplace.
There's hot apple cider in your cup.
Your cat Gracie is asleep on the sofa, and
Mozart is playing on the radio.
Even your refrigerator is humming along, while
Your finger keeps your place in a book, and
You are writing these questions to Me.

Put down your book, Sweetie.
Put down your pen.
Just for tonight, put down your questions, and
Listen to My boy Mozart."

## Grandmama God Comforts Me

Grandmama God says, "Hush child.
Stop fretting. Just for tonight.
Shhh. You're safe all the same.
When you catch yourself fretting,
Just call My name.
I'll be on the next plane.
No, I'm just teasing.
I'll be right at your side.
Better, I'll be holding you tight.
I'll take all your worries
And hurl them out in the night
To the farthest star.
You are safe in My arms.
You really are.

Then, while your mind is still,
I'll fill it with peace, Child.
So hush, Love. Shhh. Hush."

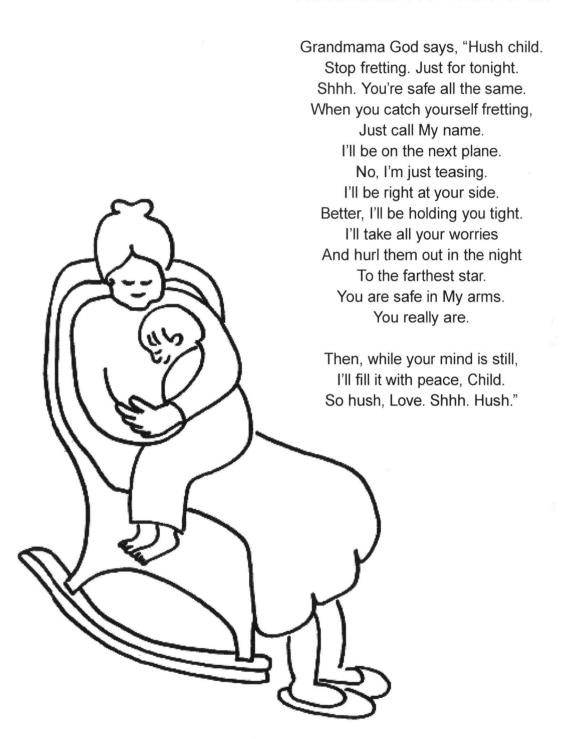

## Grandmama God Says, "You're Home"

"That's right. Relax, Child. You're home.
Tonight you had a terrible time.
I held on to you till we got home, but
You barely knew it. You mostly felt alone.
But remember? You talked to your child.
You went to the next room. You told
Those people just enough of the truth.
You stayed with yourself, Honey.
You paid attention to your feelings.
You held onto Ruth's fondness for you,
And you honored the others. You did fine.
Don't you see, Child? You did fine.
Now you'll get even better. Next time
You might call a cab and come home.

Better? Let's see what that means.
You'll come to Me right away, Love,
We'll talk it over, and fast make a
Joyful escape. Or we'll figure out
How to have fun where you are.
Mostly I'll help you feel free, not stuck
In cold soup. Honey, you spent
So much of your life with folks
Who didn't know how to play.
Now when you feel trapped like tonight,
You get jammed as an oyster.
Be polite. Be free. Be frugal. Be me.
Don't offend. Don't pretend.
Stay or leave? Stay or leave.

Your frugal self just wants to love you.
Your polite self just wants you loved.
I'm here now, Mary. I'll help you break free,
Not just free from bad evenings,
But also free from old rules.
Freedom' s close now.
You're on your way home.

Home is Love, Child, your sweet love for yourself.
And it's My love for you, reflected in yours.
You're ready to give yourself love all the time,
Whatever you choose, whatever you do.
And you're learning to say when you need to,
'I don't feel good. I want to go home.'
No one need be offended. My love will be there.

Talk this over with Ruth and your friends.
Celebrate your new freedom. I'll help you.
The truth is, you're home."

## Grandmama God, I Want One Thing

Grandmama God, You keep asking what I want.

And I keep asking myself the same question.

What do I want?

What is my heart's desire?

I finally know. Ecstasy.

That's what I want. Ecstasy.

I want to rock and roll with You all day, and

Feel the music of the spheres inside my bones.

I want to swim with You all night,

In black water under the moving moon.

In-between times, I want to be still,

Sit still like my cat Gracie,

And feel full of grace.

I want to just sit still and purr.


Thank you for asking and asking

Till I knew what I wanted.

Grandmama God, I want one thing:

Ecstasy.

## "Dream Slowly, Child," Says Grandmama God

"Dream slowly, Child.
Shhh, quiet now. No rush.
You fret and worry while you dream.
You put dreams on your back like a bag of rocks.
Dreams don't weigh a feather, Honey.
In fact, they help you fly.

You dream all in a rush; then
You feel your dreams are duties from God.
Else you get scared they're not God's will,
And you keep them secret.
Relax. Your dreams are lovely.
Granddaddy God and I love you,
Whatever you dream, whatever you do.
We just want you happy: that's all God's will is.
You and your dreams are safe with Us.

You're tired now, and afraid
You'll die if your dreams don't come true.
Hush, Sweetie. It'll all work out.
Shhh. Breathe slowly. Dream slowly.

Your sweet peace today
Will make sweeter peace tomorrow.
From today come seeds for tomorrow's blossoms.
The rest is just particulars.
So enjoy dreaming. Shhh. Relax.
No rush. No rocks. Only feathers.
Put dreams on your back like wings.
Dreams are for flying."

## "Shine Girl," Says Grandmama God

"Shine, Girl, here and now.
Go ahead and show off.
Strut your stuff. Sing your song.

I'm ready to clap loud for you.
I'll swear and shout Yahoo! for you.
It's safe to shine now, Girl.

Take a chance, Girl.
Jump on the table, do a wild dance.
I'll laugh and love it, whatever you do.
They'll love it, too.

It's time to shine, Girl.
They've waited to see you for so long.
Say what you think. Say it clear and loud.
You make Me proud.

Tell them your story.
They'll listen to every word.
You'll get all their attention.
I know you'll be well heard.

I love you, Girl. You're Mine.

## Grandmama God, I Want to Watch TV

Grandmama God, I want to be with You,
But now I really want to watch TV.
What should I do?

"Honeyplum, sweet Mary, you set up some choices
Like they're the North and South Poles.
I swear, Girl, you tickle My eternal soul.

But you're healing lovely now,
And so you come to Me with your questions.
Well, I'm turning you toward wholeness, Love, and
No more splits of earth below and heaven above.
It's all one, Dear, earth, heaven, stars, TV,
sweet potatoes, poems, red wagons
and invisible, infinite Love.

So to answer your question tonight, Mary, My Pet,
Come sit on the couch with Me.
I'll watch TV with you.
Turn on the set."

## How To Please Grandmama God

Grandmama God, I am your grateful daughter.
I want to please You.
How can I please You?

And Grandmama God says,
"Are you hungry, Child?
What would you like to eat?"

And I say, "Yes, Grandmama God,
I am very hungry.
But first tell me how to please You."

And Grandmama God says,
"No, Child, you first.
Tell me what you would like to eat."

And I say,
"What do you have, Grandmama God?
I'm sure anything You have is fine."

And Grandmama God says,
"I have everything your heart desires, My Dear.
No menu. No limit.
Close your eyes and think of
The food that would most satisfy your soul."

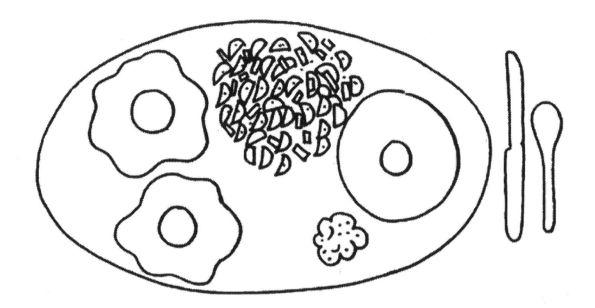

And I say, "Grandmama God,
You know I have oatmeal for breakfast every morning.
This morning I want hash brown potatoes
With onions, like my mother used to make
On Sunday mornings.
I want two eggs over easy. Hot.
And I want a rye bagel with caraway seeds, buttered,
With orange marmalade on the side.
This morning these would most satisfy my soul."

And Grandmama God says,
"Now you're talking, Honeychild.
Now you're talking how to please Me.
Please yourself, Child. Please yourself."

### *"You're The Queen Now,"*
### *Says Grandmama God*

Grandmama God, tell me how to handle
My inner critic.

"Honey, I'm glad you asked Me.
Your inner critic is a mean queen
As tall as the Empire State Building.
She's queen of blame around here.
Used to be she tried to keep you safe
But now she's power-happy, and
She keeps you feeling small and wrong.
No more. Stop her. You are her boss.
You are by nature outspoken,
Outrageous, free as a gypsy, wild.
This nagging critic has you meek and mild,
Wary as a whipped child.

Find your tongue, Woman, and
Tell this crazed critic her time is up.
It's your time now to stand tall
And be power-happy.
So dress up, be outrageous, free, and wild.
You're no longer a child.
You're the queen around here now."

## Grandmama God Gives My Critic a New Job

"I'm giving your critic a new job today, Mary.
Her nagging time has gone on too long.
You see, that critic came to keep you safe from mean authorities.
She tells you what to do, what's wrong with you,
So you'll look clean and smart when the mean ones come.

But you are safe, My Dear.
You're safe with Me.
You're safe as a robin's egg in a nest.
You're safe as a baby kangaroo.
You're in My pocket. You're in My vest.
You're in the heart of Grandmama God.

So relax, you and your critic.
Nothing and no one can harm you.
Be what you call imperfect.
Take a chance.
Your growing graceful ease
Will flow like a dance,
And your critic's new job is to tell you
You're beautiful, precious and fine
Just like you are,
No matter what anyone says.
You're My daughter. You're Mine
So Mary, I'll give you a plan--
In case your critic goes back to old fears,
You send her to Me, as fast as you can.
I'm the one she needs then,
And you come to Me, Too.
You're My chick.
I'm your ever-loving old mama hen."

## Grandmama God, I'm Tired of Being Brave

Grandmama God, I'm tired of being brave.
I'm tired of trying, sighing,
Tying and untying my sensible shoes.

"My dear Mary, My brave daughter,
What would you want to be, if not brave?"

Grandmama God, thank You for asking.
Let's see. I'd like to be spontaneous and silly,
Lighthearted and fun. You know,
Playful, earthy, wild and free,
My satisfied, laughing, monkey me.

"Ah, Baby, Child, Girl, Woman, be patient.
You're building yourself from the core.
I'm centering you, grounding you, stilling you now,
I'm glad you want more, but
Let's stay on this phase, go deeper, strike ore.
I'm mining you now, Girl.
You're pure gold at heart.

So keep on with your child talks,
Keep on walking your beach by the sea;
Keep on all your quiet times,
Keep on writing with Me.

Do all that you do to love yourself more.
Then your monkey will come,
And you'll laugh till you're sore,
In good time. Just be patient.
Give each phase its due.

Actually, I'm proud that you bought more sensible shoes.
Think what you once bought, say,
Just four years ago,
Those green shoes from Sears,
And so many shoes with high heels,
To woo non-sensible men. Look back.
Give three cheers!

Your monkey's a stretch now.
But she'll come in good time.
Go from brave to loved, Girl, that's the next step.
Tie your sensible shoes feeling loved, Mary,
Brave and well-loved Child of Mine.

## Grandmama God, I Want to Bloom Soon

Grandmama God, I want to bloom. Soon.
I've been striving and climbing
Near up to the moon.
I'm tired and weary of trying.
Please help me bloom.

Let me take one more deep breath
And pow! Kaboom! I'm a blossom,
Like a leather-pink magnolia
*With a sweet perfume.*
*Please, Grandmama God. Soon.*

*"Ooh, Mary, My daughter, My child,*
*You think you're supposed to strive*
*and sweat and climb for Me.*
*Come down from the moon, Love.*
*Stop trying to sing the perfect tune,*
*As though there were a certain*
*Way for you to prove yourself.*
*Just stop, My precious silly loon.*
*Listen to Me.*

*You think you're just leaves and stem,*
*Waiting for maybe a little bud next June.*
*You are in full bloom!*
*You are a magnificent Mary Feagan bloom.*
*Honest. Now. Your fragrance fills the room.*
*Oh, if only you could see yourself*
*As I see you, bright as the moon.*
*You'd ooh and ahhh. You'd be amazed and proud*
*Of your beauty, your luminous self in bloom."*

## Grandmama God Praises Me

"You see the sky and say
It is spectacular.
You are more wonderful than any day's sky.

You see your cat at play and say
She is delightful.
You are more delightful.
Than every cat.
You play with words; you draw.
Your words and drawings
Set Me spinning with joy whole new galaxies.

You see the children's beautiful faces.
You are in awe of such preciousness.
You are so precious, so dear to Me.
Your sweet service to them
Is a faint echo of My absolute service to you,
My own beloved and wonderful daughter."

## The Sky Love Poem From Grandmama God

"The sky you love so, loves you, too,
Mary, My radiant daughter.
You are beautiful as a morning sky.
When it sees you coming,
It glistens and grows bright for you, and
All the clouds puff out with joy.
The noon sky glows full and proud
When you look up at it, My splendid daughter.
The evening sky turns pink with pleasure
When you come to see her show.
The sky rains to serve you,
Snows to slow you down to peace.
Each day the fresh sky falls
In love with you again.
The sky only wants you to feel loved and honored,
Mary, My Radiant Splendid Sky-Daughter."

## "Honor Yourself," Says Grandmama God

"Honor yourself, My daughter," says Grandmama God.
"Don't light candles in My honor today.
Light candles in your own honor.
I already know I am Fullness of Being.
I am in ecstasy in My own Eternal Bliss.
It's time now for you to claim your fullness.
It's time you honor your own sacred self
As my child, My divine daughter,
Daughter of Eternal Bliss.

Now divine daughter, carry those candles
For your dear sacred self today.
Walk as My daughter, proud and full.
Walk tall, for you carry the light,
You carry the Fullness of Being in you."

### "Beauty Is Your Secret Name," Says Grandmama God

"Beauty is your secret name, My daughter.
You see beauty above you in the soft blue sky.
Your soft beauty is sweeter by far.
The sky's beauty is your mirror today.

Beauty is your secret name, My daughter.
You see beauty before you in the ocean waves.
You're resilient courage takes My breath away.
The majestic sea is your mirror today.

Beauty is your secret name, My daughter.
You hear beauty in the songs of birds.
Your poetry charms Me more than a world of birds.
The songs of birds are your mirror today.
Beauty is your secret name, My daughter."

## "Put Beauty On," Says Grandmama God

You're my own daughter, Mary.
Today I'll not call you 'Child.'
You're a goddess, a priestess, a woman.
You're a beautiful part of Myself.
I've put beauty above and around you.
There's even greater beauty within you.
So put beauty on.
Clothes, jewels, scarves, hats,
Wrap yourself in beauty.

Buy a great big Easter hat
With ribbons and flowers
And butterflies on it.
No, Darling Woman, don't make it,
Though I know you could.
Go buy it.
You can go back to making
When you've spoiled yourself enough.
Now it's time for store-bought beauty,
Splendid spending and spoiling
For your sweet special self.

Feel your exuberant soul filling your body,
And wear your exuberance, Woman.
Declare, flaunt, proclaim your grown-up-joy."

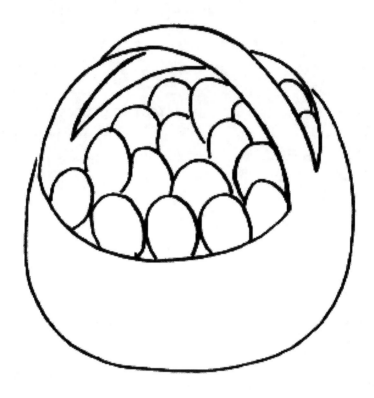

## Grandmama God Says, "It's Time"

"I'm telling you, Woman, it's time.
You've been needy and greedy for love too long.
You thought it was for a man's love, and
You put all your eggs in any man's basket.
So from now on, I'm holding your basket.
And I'm telling you, Girl, it's full of eggs."

### "Savor Yourself, Girl," Says Grandmama God

"Savor yourself, Girl," says Grandmama God.
"You are a ripe sweet juicy pear
You are fresh popcorn at a country fair.
You are a hot peach Danish roll.
You, My own daughter,
Were once on the dole
Begging men and school children
For the love you longed for,
Your sweet right,
While your own air
Whistled its delight with you.
Of course, I've been whistling, too.
Girl, you melt in my mouth
Like peppermint ice cream.
You're a grandmama's dream come true.
Savor yourself, Girl, do.
Slow down long enough
To enjoy your own essential charm.
You are more delicious
Than pecan pie a la mode, warm."

## Grandmama God Says, "Come Home To Yourself"

"Come home to yourself now, Girl.
It's ten o'clock. Listen. Look.
The world's soft and black. Hey, Honey,
Don't be listening to Yugoslavia and Iraq.
Come home to yourself now.
Listen to your heart, your bones.
Forget I said the world at all.
You're safe now. Make yourself at home.
It's safe to forget everything outside,
Though you'd be safe out there, too.
You'd be safe riding a camel in Timbuktu.
You'd be safe walking a path in Palestine.
You're safe in the middle of life or death.
'Know why, dear Mary? Because you're Mine.

So hush, Child, relax. You're fine.
You're safe. You're Mine. Come home."

## Grandmama God, I Want to Sing Your Song

Grandmama God, I want to sing Your song,
Even if some say I'm wrong.
I want to sing Your song,
And hear it answered clear and strong.
I want to lead a throng of people to You,
and we all together sing along, Grandmama God.
We all together sing to You a loud and lovely song.

## I Am Grandmama God

I'm just beginning to feel it,
As I heal and my heart grows:
I am Grandmama God.
I have given birth to myself, yes,
That was wondrous enough.
My sweet self was born from my old self with
Grandmama God hovering over me,
Loving me, guiding me,
As I tended myself, myself Her dear child.
As I learned to walk, sometimes fly,
She was always close by.

Now this new birth is beginning.
I just felt the first clue
As I put clean sheets on the bed for my friend.
Grandmama God wasn't hovering this time.
Rather, my hands were Her hands.
My joy was one with the joy of Grandmama God.
Not two. Not my joy and Hers.
Just one delight.
Just for a moment I felt and I knew:
I am Grandmama God.

Printed in the United States
by Baker & Taylor Publisher Services